Becoming
Who I Am

Becoming
Who I Am

Reflections on Wholeness and
Embracing Our Divine Stories

BETH-SARAH WRIGHT

Morehouse Publishing
NEW YORK

"I am Who I am in the eyes of God, nothing more and nothing less."

—Saint Francis

To my family, whose love and presence inspire
me every day to become who I am.

Morehouse Publishing, 19 East 34th Street, New York, NY 10016

Morehouse Publishing is an imprint of Church Publishing Incorporated.
www.churchpublishing.org

Cover design by Laurie Klein Westhafer
Typeset by Rose Design

Library of Congress Cataloging-in-Publication Data

Wright, Beth-Sarah.
 Becoming who I am : reflections on wholeness and embracing our divine stories / Beth-Sarah Wright.
     pages cm
 ISBN 978-0-8192-3179-6 (pbk.) -- ISBN 978-0-8192-3180-2 (ebook)
1. Older Christians--Religious life. 2. Aging--Religious aspects--Christianity.
3. Nicene Creed--Miscellanea. 4. Numbers in the Bible. 5. Forty (The number)--Miscellanea. 6. African American women--Religious life. I. Title.
 BV4580.W75 2015
 248.8'43--dc23

                                   2015010036

Printed in the United States of America

contents

INTRODUCTION
Symbolon

Our stories anchor us. They are integral to who we are and to who we become. They give our lives meaning and make us each human. They connect us. While they strengthen us, inspire us, and encourage us as we traverse this unpredictable journey of life, they can also hinder us and hold us back from truly becoming the people we are meant to be. Our stories matter and telling our stories can break down barriers, open doors, and bring freedom, liberation, and even healing. So why do we have such difficulty in telling our stories?

Perhaps we are silenced because of our pride and egos, or our pain and disappointments, or shame and embarrassment. Maybe we think it's too uncomfortable to be vulnerable like that. Recognizing just how common our stories are, however, frees us to share them. As God's children, God's extensions here on Earth, we ultimately all share the same story, God's story. And when we say yes to that story, we realize that all of our individual stories—regardless of our unique journeys—connect, reflect, and point to that one story.

This book offers Jesus's story as a real-life mirror to our own stories, ultimately making God's story, our story, and our story, God's story. For nearly all my life, every Sunday at church I, along with millions around the world, recite the Nicene Creed, Jesus's story, as a statement of what we believe. It is a story we profess as the embodiment of our faith. But how do these words penetrate into the messiness of our real lives? How does this story help us to make sense of our own individual stories? The Greek word for creed is *symbolon*, which means half of a broken object which, when placed together with the other half, verifies the bearer's identity, or two halves of a whole. I want to fill my brokenness with Jesus's story. Such that my story becomes Jesus's and Jesus's story becomes mine. I want to wholly live into my identity. I want to become who I am. And that is what this book is about. Aligning our stories with Jesus's story. Telling our stories in such a way that imitates and becomes one with God's Magnum Opus, the ultimate story of grace, mercy, hope, healing, joy, and victory. *Becoming Who I Am* encourages us to embrace and tell our whole stories and to discover our divine capacity for true life transformation and joy!

Introduction

I use 8 moments in the Nicene Creed to give new meaning to real-life circumstances of identity, pain, family life, dealing with depression, and healing. When we do this—seek to embody Jesus's story—we are able to see our life events and experiences differently with the template of Jesus's story overlaying them. We feel differently—grateful, hopeful, liberated, and empowered, especially when we recognize our own divine potential and capacity—our divine stories. And finally, we act differently, choosing new ways of being in the world and exercising our power to write the endings of our stories, no matter where they began or have taken us.

I recently turned 40, a pivotal age for many. Our bodies begin to talk back to us in rather intriguing ways. We become reflective about where we are in our lives. We ask, is this where I want to be? Is this who I want to be? When I turned 40, I was overwhelmed with gratitude. Gratitude for being alive, because in my darkest moments I wanted to end my life. Gratitude for God's grace—free and unmerited—for showing me that light can break through the darkness, that joy and healing are possible and that I can experience the miracle of laughter once again. Grateful that each new day is an opportunity to love God more, love myself more, and to love others more. To my surprise, turning 40 marked a new beginning for me. I still had questions and doubt, but I did not ask them the same way. The questions were more filled with possibility and excitement and above all, hope.

In the Bible the number 40, from Jesus being sent out into the wilderness for 40 days to the 40 years of God's people roaming the desert, represents periods of trial and revelatory clarity, leading to renewal and revival. In other words, turning 40 is a beginning not an ending! That is a word many of us can hold onto! That is why the book consists of 40 spiritual reflections. Ultimately, however, we can by partnering with God transform each age, each period in our lives to be moments of new beginnings.

Begotten.

    Light from Light.

        And Was Made Woman.

            Suffering Death.

                Rising Again.

                    In Accordance with the Stories.

                        Giver of Life.

                            Life of the World to Come.

Introduction

How will you live your life in the world to come?
Me? I want to become who I am!

PART 1

Begotten

OUR BEGINNING

Our stories begin with our divine creation.

Enhanced and developed by our birthplace, our

upbringing, our families. We grow. We change.

We experience.

Change remains constant. God remains unchanged.

No matter what, we are enough! All that we need,

by God's dream, is already bundled

in our human flesh.

Trust it. Access it. Learn from it. Rest in it.

3

ON THIS DAY . . .

The sweet waters of baptism wash over me
God calls to me and gives me hope
And I have a new life in Jesus Christ!

On this day
He takes my hand and walks with me as I grow
He teaches me his ways and I will joyfully follow him
He forgives me and gives me a clean heart!

On this day
All who stand with me,
Promise to show me the light
And I will shine for all to see!

Thank you, God, for this day and for this new chance
to know you, to serve you, and to love you more!

"By baptism . . . we too might walk in newness of life."
(Romans 6:4)

DIS A WHO WI BE!
(Dis a who *Mi* be!)

Wi likkle but wi tallawah!

Brought here in chains from the African land of our
mothers and fathers;

Wi fight di good fight; wi fierce and wi powerful; and
wid cunning and resistance we run run run away to di
mountaintops and survive, thrive, and live in freedom
We are di maroons of Suriname, Jamaica, Barbados;
we are the inimitable Queen Nanny, leader of the
maroons; A woman who when she a fight di British
man she catch di bullets dem inna her bottom and
den spit dem back out!

Dis a who wi be!

We remember di Black Jacobins; Toussaint L'Ouver-
ture in Haiti with his African spirit who fought the
British, the French, and the Americans and won! The
First independent black republic in the world.

Dis a who wi be!

Den come wi Emancipation! Independence! Good-
bye Union Jack; Hello to di red, black, and white flag

of Trinidad and Tobago and di rising sun in di blue, white, and black flag of Antigua and Barbuda.

Colours dat speak to di energy of di sun and sea and lands
Colours dat speak to di strength, purpose, and unity of a unique people
Colours dat speak to a new national identity. Black, Chinese, Indian, Syrian, Dougla; Out of many, One people!
Wi speak di H-inglish, Patois, Dutch, Español, Français, Papamiento, Creole; our language, our words, our existence; "sak passé, nah boule!"

Dis a who wi be!

Wi remember di African riddims dat live deep inna wi belly, inna wi hips; inna wi waist and we dance yes wi dance away wi pain wid di limbo, mento, Ska; we whine a new existence wid wi carnival; Jouvet! Jouvet! Wid di soca, calypso, zouk, rip saw, chutney music; dancehall and di reggae

Yes! reggae mi dis and reggae mi dat!

Dis a who wi be!

Wi remember di words of Aimé Césaire, Léon Damas et les autres qui vient de les isles que parle le français comme Guadeloupe et Martinique et French Guyana. Writers, poets, intellectuals who raised up la Négritude—the acceptance, appreciation, and celebration of the historical and cultural experience of all black people.

Wi listen to di stories of Brer Anancy and Brer Rabbit who teach us creative and ingenious ways of surviving inna dis ya world.

Dis a who wi be!

Wi remember di power of singer Bob Marley; Pan-Africanist Marcus Garvey; Nobel Laureate Derek Walcott; philosopher C. L. R. James; legendary cricketers Sir Garfield Sobers and Brian Lara; revolutionary Walter Rodney; writer V. S. Naipaul; poet and national heroine, The Honorable Louise Bennett or Miss Lou; healer during the Crimean War, nurse Mary Seacole; defender and heroine of Methodism in Barbados, Sarah Ann Gill; we remember all these and many many more who spread the infectious riddims of our Caribbean spirit to the farthest corners of the world.

Dis a who wi be!

Wi remember when di Maroons dig di holes inna di ground and cover dem to cook di meat so the smoke would not rise and reveal dem hiding place and we get jerk! Jerk pork, jerk fish, jerk chicken; we remember di sweetness of sapodilla, naseberry, pomerac, otaheite apple, mangoes—julie mango, number 11 mango, black skin mango, East Indian mango; yes we remember callaloo, rice pelau, curry goat, curry chicken, mannish water good fi yu dawta; paw paw balls, roti; coconut bake; banana fritter, conch fritter, saltfish fritter; and of course di sweet, sweet, sweet dumpling.

Dis a who wi be!

Wi remember di indomitable spirit of Jah! We are Catholic, Methodist, Seven Day Adventist, Anglican; We are Hindu, Muslim, Rastafari, Vodun, Pocomania, Obeah; Dese are all o di ways we talk about dis one God who created us; dis one God who placed us in the sun-kissed islands nestled in crystal blue waters and glistening white sand; Yes dis one God who strengthens us and gives us hope and courage in the face of our challenges; Dis one God who made us likkle but tallawah!

Tank you God! Bon Ye Bon, Jah Live! God is good!

Dis a who wi be! Dis a who wi be! Dis a who wi be!

SOUNDS OF HOME

This poem was inspired by my mother who told me that when she first went to live abroad in England she could not sleep because it was too quiet! There were no sounds of the crickets singing at night in the bushes. No familiar sounds of home.

Having lived myself outside of Jamaica since I was 15, I too often think of these sounds of home.

And so I dedicate this poem to my mother and to Miss Lou, our national poet, who always performed her poetry in Jamaican *patois*, the inimitable sound of home.

You may not understand everything but that's ok. Just listen to the rhythms and the cadence of the words. These are my sounds of home.

———————

But is what yu a tell mi? Yu seh dat di pitty pitty gyal dem a sussu pon mi?
Eh Eh! Cheeeuuups!
Mi no like dat at all. Dem should a know betta!
Cick cick cick
Dem tink seh me come a foreign and den figet bout where mi come from.

But mek mi tell yu someting, mi remembah everything because it inna mi head, inna mi blood, inna mi bone.

Mi remembah di machete a *cheng cheng* a cut down di sweet sugarcane and a *shing* cross di coconut to pour out di cool cool water.
Mi remembah di *swish swish* of the seawater on
the soft sand early inna di morning under di radiant
   sunrise
Mi remembah di *budumbup* of di mango dem a drop
   pon mi rooftop
Mi remembah di chorus of di cricket dem singing at
   nighttime inna di bushes

Yes mi remembah because it inna mi head, inna mi blood, inna mi bone.

Mi remembah mi mama seh "*pull han*" when mi
reach inna di pot to steal a sweet dumpling
Mi remembah di man a sell *peanutsssss peanutssss,*
   wrigleys fruitella peanutsssss
Mi remembah when di bredren a play football
dem seh "*pass di ball!*" "*No man a wha yu a do?*"
Salaaad! Goooaaal!!!
Mi remembah pon di bus dem shout "*one stop driver!*
Let me off ya so!"

And when dem a play dominoes mi remembah when
dem seh *"How much card yu have? A who I gwine
sop tonight? Serve mi a Heineken! Heineken!
  Heineken!!!"*

Yes, mi remembah because it inna mi head, inna mi blood, inna mi bone

Mi remembah di riddim of the sound system a *mm
  mm mm* inna di distance
Mi remembah di *ping ping* and di *pong pong* of the
  rain a fall pon di zinc roof top
Mi remembah di *squis squis squis* of the clothes a
  wash pon di river bed

Yes mi remembah because it inna mi head, inna mi blood, inna mi bone

Mi remembah because mi know seh it important to
  me to feel like meself
Mi remembah because it make me feel whole inside
Mi remembah because di riddims dat move mi body,
dat move deep inna mi hips, inna mi belly come from
one place, one sweet sweet place, a place dat mi
would never figet and dat deh place mi call *home*.
A place where mi cyan remembah mi.
Inna mi head, inna mi blood, inna mi bone.

WHAT DO YOU DO WITH GOD'S DREAM FOR YOU?

When God appeared to Moses,
Wild bush enflamed
God had a dream for him
A dream of being a savior, a ruler
A dream of freedom and of parting waters

Yet even with this dream from the lips of God,
Doubt poured from Moses's mouth,
"Who am I to lead the people out of Egypt?"

What do YOU do with God's dream for you?

And when God's people roamed the fertile
land God dreamed for them
After shackles fell from their ankles and wrists
and columns of fire protected them
Words of ingratitude fell from their lips
"If only the Lord had killed us back in Egypt."

What do YOU do with God's dream for you?

When Jesus, bare feet resting on water,
Calls to Peter, "Don't be afraid. Take courage.
I am here."
Peter steps out but soon succumbs to the fear
of strong wind and waves and begins to sink.
"Save me, Lord!" he pleads.

With arm outstretched, Jesus says, "You have
so little faith, why did you doubt me?"

What do YOU do with God's dream for you?

When God whispers to a blade of grass to
"grow,"
Does the blade answer "No, Not I"?

When the fowls of the air hunger in their belly
Do they cry out in fear?

Consider the lilies of the field and how they
grow; They don't work or make their clothing
yet are resplendent in their glorious array.
Consider the wounded wild animal, how it
heals, restores, recovers in God's hands
and in God's time

Consider the dream God has for you

Pay attention

Listen for God's dream

Embrace God's dream.

Live into God's dream!

A DREAM PRAYER

God, may your dream for me become my life.

Selah!

PART 2

Light from Light

I AM THE LIGHT

When I was about 13 years old and would have bad dreams and couldn't sleep, my father would open the small Bible I had at my bedside to Psalm 27. He said, "Before you put your head on the pillow, read this psalm and you will not be afraid. 'The Lord is my light and my salvation; whom shall I fear? The Lord is the stronghold of my life; of whom shall I be afraid?'" I still remember the calm that would flow over my body as I would lay my head down and close my eyes. It was so reassuring, so empowering. For many years, that may have been the only part of Scripture I read! It accompanied me in the days my soul yearned and hungered for my home when first I lived abroad in Scotland. It brought me confidence before every audition for a school play or before performing a poem on stage. It reassured me before taking a final exam. It flew with me on every airplane, to places like San Juan, Puerto Rico, where I lived and worked as a waitress and artist just so I could learn Spanish; to places like Cambridge, England, where I would not only have my first academic publication, but would meet a man walking down the street who would become my husband and father to my children. It pilfered its way into the operating room when I lay on my back awaiting C-sections to welcome our children into the world.

"The Lord is my LIGHT and my salvation." With this light, the light of God, there is no room for fear. There is no room for darkness. And because we are all children of God, we have this light too! We have the awesome opportunity and indeed responsibility to shine this light; in our very beings; in our words, our thoughts, our actions. It pierces darkness with such ease and so little is needed to make a difference. But sometimes we find that we stifle our own light, desperately squelching it with self-doubt, low self-esteem, lack of self-worth. And yes, others may also try with harsh words and loveless tones to extinguish our light. But the ingenious thing about that divine light is that it yearns to shine, it longs to be seen. No matter what, the light remains, unwavering. Light will always make a way. Let it be free. It is contagious, you know. Let your light shine!

———————

"Keep your eyes open, your lamp burning, so you don't get musty and murky. Keep your life as well-lighted as your best-lighted room." (Luke 11:33–36)

In memory of my father, Keith Panton (November 2, 1935—February 18, 2015), whose light shines perpetually in our hearts.

DARE TO BE DIFFERENT

"Dare to be different and to follow your own star." Growing up, these words were written on a poster hung in my room. They were particularly encouraging being the only sister of two older brothers before my baby sister came along 6 years later. And they were important in learning how to thrive, not just survive, in the fishbowl in which my family lived. You see, I grew up in a small town in the cool hills of Mandeville, Jamaica, where my father was not only the first Jamaican CEO of a large multinational company, but also a priest in the Anglican church; and where my mother was not only a consummate host and partner to my father, but the matron of the hospital, president of the PTA for as long as I can remember, and an immaculate voice on the national radio. They gave "ubiquitous" new meaning! Many eyes were on my family and that meant certain expectations and often misguided assumptions about who we were. "Daring to be different and following my own star" seemed to be an ideal way of finding my own voice separate and apart from other's expectations of me.

"Daring to be different" meant graduating from high school at 15 to attend a boys' school in Edinburgh, Scotland. Four hundred boys and 20 girls! And the only black girl there. "Daring to be different" meant being one of the first girls to join the school's Scottish army to become a lance corporal. "Daring to be different" meant travelling to faraway places like Cyprus, Egypt, and Israel to discover more of this remarkable world.

Taking risks and following the road less travelled were certainly some ways to follow my own star, but as I grew older I encountered the astonishing fact that the star was not really my own, but God's. And it became clearer and clearer that if I let go of where I think (and truth be told "want") my star should go, *the* star will lead me in the direction I am supposed to go. *My* star didn't matter as much anymore as *the* star became more apparent.

"Thy will be done," Mary said when she was told she would be the mother to a son who would be called the Christ. Talk about daring to be different! Here was an unwed teenaged girl, visited by an angel sent by God who tells her quite unexpectedly that she is to be the mother to the Messiah. And in the face of this grave uncertainty, fear, and the potential of persecution by her family and her betrothed, this young woman, with courage, says yes to God! When I came to fully grasp all of what that meant, daring to be different took on completely new meaning!

Daring to be different means moving beyond the fear to embrace possibility. Daring to be different means listening, being still and listening. Daring to be different means recognizing purpose and meaning. Daring to be different means seeing God in everything, even in the uncertainty of life. Daring to be different means becoming more fully who we are. Daring to be different means offering ourselves to be the difference/create a difference/see a difference in the world. Daring to be different means partnering with and following a new star, God's star.

An Excerpt from the Talmud

Live each day to the fullest. Get the most from each hour, each day. and each age of your life. Then you can look forward with confidence and back without regret. Be yourself, but be your best self! Dare to be different and to follow your own star. And don't be afraid to be happy. Enjoy what is beautiful. Love with all your heart and soul.

SEND ME

I heard the voice of the Lord saying, "Whom shall I send, and who will go for us?" Then I said, "Here I am; send me." (Isaiah 6:8)

Lord, I unite with you to be an instrument of
confidence, conviction, and courage for myself,
in my family, my community and in the world.

As I arise taking the first breath of the day
and opening my eyes to a glorious sunrise, I come
into the morning aware of your presence, your grace,
and your blessing of life.

As I begin this day, I go to my special place to be
with you, to spend time alone with you, where I may
praise you, draw closer to you, and listen to you
through your word and prayer.

I go into the shower to cleanse, care for, embrace, and
celebrate my beautiful body, this God-given temple.

I go to my beloved with an open and clean heart,
a giving soul, and a forgiving spirit,
with faithfulness and patience, wisdom and true

godliness, so that our home may be a haven
of blessing and peace.

I embrace the children who have been entrusted
in my care with love and laughter, so that I may
rightly see their divinity.

I go to the breakfast table to nourish and strengthen
my body for your service.

Lord, I go out into the world so that others may see
you in all that I say, do, and accomplish today.

I go to my place of service; confident in the gifts
you have blessed me with, to be an effective
steward of them.

I go to those who are alone and who have no one
to care for them. I am empowered with your
graciousness of spirit to share with them the time,
talent, and treasure you have shared with me.

I go to my enemies with a forgiving heart to be an
agent of reconciliation and peace.

Lord, I go to my spiritual home to worship and
adore you and to be filled by you.

I return to my home at night able to leave
all the weariness and stresses of the day outside
my doorstep.

I walk into my home, to friends and to family and
am recharged and comforted in their embrace.

I sit at the dinner table knowing that I eat because
of your mercy, grace, and generosity.

I watch the evening news understanding that
you have the whole world in your hands.

I go to bed knowing that you are the only giver
of true rest.

I close my eyes and go to the dream world in hopes
that your dream for me may become my life.

I'll go, Lord. Send me!

PART 3

And Was Made Woman

AND WAS MADE WOMAN . . .

I. (Our Belief)

We believe in our God
Our Mother-Father God
Our refuge
Our stronghold,
Our rock

We honor our elders leaning on the lives of our
    God-sisters,
We lean on Sarah, Mary, Esther, Naomi, Ruth,
Elizabeth, Mary Magdalene, and others
We lean on all those who came before us, our
enslaved foremothers, our freedom fighters,
    our trailblazers
We learn from them, we carry their wisdom on our
shoulders, and we pass their powerful legacy onto
our God-daughters.

We support, encourage, embrace, raise up, build up,
hold up our sons, our men
Let me say that again!
We support, encourage, embrace, raise up, build up,
hold up our sons, our men.

For we know that the work of Moses, Noah, Jesus,
and many others yesterday, today and tomorrow
Has been strengthened by the power and presence
   of women.
Remember we were "Last at the cross, first at the tomb."

II. (Our Oblation)

We embrace, believe in, and nurture our children,
    our youth.
We are mothers, blood mothers, other mothers;
    stepmothers, adoptive mothers;
Aunties, grandmas, great grandmas, big sisters;
We love, encourage, and support our children
    for haven't you heard?
"Out of the mouths of babes and sucklings, praise
    has been perfected!"

We know we are sinners
We forgive ourselves
We forgive ourselves
We forgive others
We let go and we let God.

We *believe* in God's justice
We believe in *God's* justice
We believe in God's *justice.*

III. (Our Beauty)

Our lips shout for joy when we sing praises to the Lord!
We sing
We laugh
We drink tea!
We love our food!
We weep, we break our hearts, we hug, we hope,
   we heal.
We dance
We sway our hips
We walk in that certain kind of way!
With a little sass, a little shimmer!
We strut with God's confidence running up our spines!

        We are beautiful!

        We are beautiful!

        We are beautiful!

IV. (Our Prayer)

When we are afraid, when we are worried, when
   we are faced with life's valleys;
When the waters have come up to our necks
and we sink deep in the mire, where there is no
   foothold . . .

We look to the young teenaged girl over two thou-
sand years ago, who was visited by an angel and told
that she would be a mother to a son who would be
called the Christ; we look to this young mother who,
with a deep and abiding faith, simply said in response
to this news,
"Be it unto me according to thy word"
Thy will be done!

And we pray, yes, we pray!

We pray with a vengeance; we become prayer
   warriors.

We pray with a boldness because we know that if we
"Ask it will be given, if we search we will find and if
we knock, the door will be opened!"

For with God nothing is impossible!

We affirm the Holy Spirit in our lives guiding our every move, our every decision, our every waking moment, we give our lives over to him.

Praise be to God, Praise be to God, Praise be to God!

BALANCING

. . . As far as I have read in Scripture, I don't ever remember Jesus saying "Go forth and burn yourself out! Be frantic! Run around like a chicken with your head chopped off! . . . Neglect your family. Neglect your work. Neglect yourself." Do you? Yet in many instances we find that we do. And we yearn for a peace, a sense of wholeness. Not to be supermen and women but simply to handle our day-to-day responsibilities in a way that is kind to ourselves, to others around us, and that follows God. Jesus does ask us not to worry, "for who by worrying can add a single hour to his or her life?"

. . . In the story of Mary and Martha (Luke 10:38–42), Jesus doesn't say anything about "balancing." He clearly says put him first. Put God first. But how, Martha might ask, or we might ask when we still have children to tend to, toilets to clean, laundry to be done, dishes to wash, briefs to write, patients to attend to, work projects to finish; we still have our bodies to take care of, significant others to love and validate, friends and parents who want our presence. The list goes on and on no matter where we are in our lives.

How? By choosing to say yes to God. Wholly, completely, and freely. We have a choice. There is no prescriptive way of being today's woman, there are only descriptive ways, and we have a choice as people of faith to create these for ourselves while honoring what we know God ultimately expects of us.

To choose to say yes to God means saying yes to the fruits of living by the Spirit . . .

Love . . . of self, of others (even our enemies), of God

Joy . . . within, enduring, contagious

Peace . . . no such thing as perfection—instead possibility, persistence, and purpose. Rest in that!

Patience . . . no such thing as failure, only opportunity

Kindness . . . be reflective, be truthful, empathize

Generosity . . . born from gratitude for all parts of our stories

Faithfulness . . . see God in it all!

Gentleness . . . otherwise known as kind candor

Self-control . . . need I say more?

You choose!

GOD'S REFLECTION

When we say yes to God, we see God's reflection in our children's eyes, in their faces, and we believe that God knitted every morsel of their bodies together in their mother's womb, every cell, every vein, every muscle, uniquely, fearfully, and wonderfully made. When we say yes to God, we don't focus on their challenges, troublesome behavior (although we certainly recognize troublesome behavior!), poor choices, teenage angst. . . . Instead we celebrate the God in them. Not only did God create this being, he declares that he knows the plans for this gift of a child, plans for welfare and not for evil, plans to give a future and a hope. For you see the children may have come through our bodies, or raised by our hands, in our hearts, and in our homes, but they ultimately belong to God. The poet Khalil Gibran put it this way "Your children are not your children. They are the sons and daughters of Life's longing for itself. They come through you but not from you, And though they are with you yet they belong not to you." Knowing this reminds us that God has a plan and a purpose for each of these children; we just have to open our eyes, be patient, see, and help to discover that purpose.

WHAT'S IN A NAME?

A good name is to be chosen rather than great riches.
(Proverbs 22:1)

My name is Hadassah:

I am young; I am in the Spring of my life; beautiful, with great promise ahead of me; brimming with confidence and obtaining favor in the sight of all who look upon me. My name is Hadassah.

My name is Esther:

Mature; in the Summer of my life; I know what I believe; I know what I stand for; I am convicted by justice, by what is right; I am not afraid; I stand up for a whole people and speak for those who cannot speak for themselves. My name is Esther.

What is your name?

My name is Ruth:

I am loyal; I am determined; I am whole: I am in the Autumn of my life; I am a widow yet I am whole; I am committed to family; I live with integrity; I am whole; Where you go I go and where you stay I stay;

Your people will be my people and your God my God. My name is Ruth.

My name is Jairus's daughter:

I lay with disease in my body; lifeless; no breath; yet I can hear Jesus calling me, saying to me "Rise." He stretches out his hand and like a phoenix out of the fire I rise. I believe in a healing God; A God of grace; And like the woman diseased with the issue of blood, my faith makes me whole. I am not dead, I am only asleep. My name is Jairus's daughter.

What is your name?

My name is Sarah:

In the Winter of my life now; I carry a barren womb but not an empty heart; Just when there were no more leaves on the trees, and the ground was frozen, God let the warmth of the sunlight in and gave me a son. I believe in a merciful God, a giver of life. My name is Sarah.

My name is Jochebed:

I give birth to a male child in a time of persecution and fear. And I love him, and want to protect him and would do anything to do just that. So I clothe him in prayer and send him away knowing he will come back to me. For with God nothing is impossible. My name is Jochebed, mother of Moses.

My name is Pharoah's daughter:

I see an innocent child in a basket, I draw him out of the water and into my heart. He comes not from my body, yet he is every part of my soul. I believe in a God who takes us all as his children and we call him Abba, Father. My name is Pharoah's daughter, mother of Moses.

What is your name?

My beautiful sisters, my daughters, my girlfriends, my mothers, my grandmothers, we recognize the power in a name. There are so many names we have in the Bible and elsewhere in the tributaries of our lives that we strive to embody, emulate, live into, aspire toward, and celebrate. Yet others and truth be told, we too continue to misname ourselves, our bodies, our beings—wonderfully and fabulously made.

Who inspires you? Whose names do you seek to remember, bask in, and become your own? Who are the living, breathing women, walking among us, angels squeezed into beautiful human flesh whom we look to, lean on, learn from?

Just to set the record straight . . .

Our name is powerful; confident; strong, gifted; our name is praise, wisdom, dignity, humility; our name is charity, peace; our name is beautiful, sassy, desirable, sensual; our name is worthy, obedience; grace; joy; kindness; faithfulness; our name is courageous, forgiven, worthy, bold, partner, supporter, believer; lover; our name is change-maker, our name is generous.

Our name is beloved!

We have a name that is worth far more than rubies and diamonds;

our name is blessed, our name is blessed,
our name is blessed;

And we are highly favored!

And Jesus asked him, "What is your name?" (Mark 5:9)

PART 4

Suffering Death

GOOD FRIDAY NARRATIVES

Not strong enough
Not smart enough
Not rich enough
Not powerful enough
Not bold enough
Not brave enough
Not beautiful enough.

It's my fault.
I am awful.
I am weak.
I. Hate. Myself.

Shame. Humiliation. Naked. Ugly.
At. Wits. End.
I want to die.

I just want to find my voice
I don't know which way to turn
And the tears sit perched ready to fall
This violent impulse awaits the right trigger

I need to vomit. Not ill. Poison. Blackened my
insides. Churning. Putrid. Festering. The current

is strong and the dam can no longer hold it back.
I need to vomit.

Help.

HOLY SATURDAY MOMENTS

From time to time we are all tempted to give up and crumble under the lack of hope. But we are given an awesome gift! The gift of Jesus's resurrection! Knowing that he lives gives us the strength to live through our "Holy Saturday Moments." Those moments when our own resurrections are uncertain and our future outcomes remain suspended.

Holy Saturday is that space in between loss and hope, where we don't know if we will ever grasp joy again. In that space we are called to show up, to stand up, and to look up. In this space, in our soul valley, we bear the discomfort and stand in dry, deserted places while the wind and bulrushes strip away our ego and power and identity.

Yes, in these uncomfortable if not downright painful spaces, we are urged to draw close to, desperately hold onto, and embrace God. In these spaces we must seek out courage, grasp onto our convictions, and allow the confidence that God "will not fail us or forsake us" to fill up our spines and hold us upright as we crawl, walk, run toward the light of hope.

How do you live your "Holy Saturday Moments"?

DREAM CONSERVATION

Prayer is the thread that weaves together the tapestry
of God's wildest dreams for us.

Pray more, pray with a vengeance,
pray with boldness.
In everything, pray. Pray unceasingly, with every
word, with every breath, with every action. Rejoice
evermore. In everything give thanks, for this is the
will of God in Christ Jesus concerning you.

Prayer is response

Say

Be

Live

Prayer

And when you can't pray. When the pain silences
you. When there are no words.
Only tears. Weakened body. Heavy tongue.

Dream endangered.

With moans and groans and aching sighs,
the Spirit prays.

Dream protected.

Dream saved.

The dream lives!

———————————

Likewise the Spirit helps us in our weakness; for we do not know how to pray as we ought, but that very Spirit intercedes with sighs too deep for words. And God, who searches the heart, knows what is the mind of the Spirit, because the Spirit intercedes for the saints according to the will of God. (Romans 8:26–27)

THE BLACK MOREL

My heart aches for lives and souls lost. For being blind to human dignity. For seeing with our molded, manipulated imaginations and not with our hearts. For losing to fear and not to courage.

My heart aches, for these actions burn like wildfire. Rampant. Reckless. Contagious. Destructive. Debilitating. Deadly.

Yet, fire is not victorious.

My heart surges for the fertile medium that remains. Scorched yet not silent. Incinerated but not extinguished.

Cremated but not breathless.

Ablaze but not barren.

For up out of the gravid soil, life struggles to emerge. Bold. Defiant. Dauntless. A fire-eating delicacy bursts through.

Beautiful in its complicated brokenness.

Stalwart and assured.

Open.

Breathing in and out new possibility.

Hope.

The black morel is an edible mushroom, a delicacy that grows in massive quantities only in areas scorched by wildfires.

PART 5

Rising Again

A SPIRITUAL CRESCENDO

God has dealt bountifully with me
All my life I sing to God as long as I live
Songs of praise
Thanksgiving
As prayer
For God's wonderful reversals

I sing to remember
To forget
To grieve
To mourn
To forgive
To interpret

I sing in spirit
In mind
In body
In purpose
In action

I sing to build up
To build on
To reveal

To reflect
To respond

I sing to empower
To endure

I sing to become who I am

All my life long I'll praise God, singing songs to my God as long as I live. (Psalm 146:2)

A NEW SONG

There is a rhythm to life . . . one that connects to memories of home; a riddim that enlivens every step; a distant beat that remembers; the sun kissing our skin on the first precious days of spring!

I cannot imagine a world without this cadence, this pulse; pumping life and love and joy and spirit and hope through the courses of our veins.

But sometimes, we find ourselves curled up like scared pups on a cold night, rocking to a silent lullaby; ears unable to hear that life-giving tempo; and we fall, fall deep into a desolate pit; and when this pit of life gets deeper and deeper and stranger and stranger. . . .

A soft whisper sings

Wade in the water.
Wade in the water, children.
Wade in the water
God's gonna trouble the water

But that's when the memory of our people come; trudging through; fleeing from; captured; forced out of; taken away into new places; strange places; strange lands; strange smells; strange fruit hanging from poplar trees;

How the wicked carried us away to captivity; required from us a song; How can we sing the Lord's song in a strange land?

How can we sing a new song, our home song; our first song; our first tongue, in a strange land?

Here in this strange bed of fertile soil; roots of imagination and creativity strengthen and creep into our souls like tentacles in desperate search for nourishment. Peeling away the veil from our eyes; there is a new vision; new sight; foresight; insight.

Up out of the miry bog; secure upon a rock; patiently waiting for God to plant a new song in our mouths.

If I had the wings of a dove; if I had the wings of a dove

I would fly, fly away, fly away, and be at rest.

But since I have no wings; I cannot fly fly fly;

Since I have no wings Since I have no wings I'm gonna sing sing sing!

Since I have no wings to take me away from the fear, the dread, the pain, the sadness, to deliver me from the woundedness; the brokenness; I'm gonna sing sing sing!

Sing a new song
Dance a new dance
Shake a new shiver
Hum a new tune
Laugh a new laugh
Smile a new smile
Hit a new beat
Walk with a new stride
Whine a new whine
Hear a new rhythm
Chant a new prayer
Because *there is* a balm in Gilead to make the wounded whole . . .

Because God's goodness and mercy chases after me
My cup runneth over!
Because my soul's been anchored in the Lord
My cup runneth over!

Because he walks/runs/slides and even shuffles with me
My cup runneth over!

Because my pit becomes a palace
Praise him with trumpet and sound!
Because my obstacles are opportunities
Praise him with tambourine and dance!

Praise him with strings and pipe and organ
Praise him with clanging cymbals
Let everything that breathes; every one; every tune;
every moan; every groan; praise him! Praise him!
Praise the Lord!!!

PART 6

In Accordance with the Stories

WORSHIP

We are on a journey to wholeness.

The difference between being whole and having a hole in your soul is simply a "W."

A "w" for worship.

The question is,

What story do you worship?

What story do you choose to be filled by?

It's your choice. Choose well.

OUR STORIES MATTER

"Open our lips, Lord, and our mouths shall proclaim your praise; what is whispered in your ear in the darkness, shout it from the rooftops!" What if, when we encounter others, each of us were to see beyond that which we believe is real—which are only figments of our manipulated, maneuvered, and molded imaginations anyway—to see what is truly real—the divine deeply embedded in our DNA? And when we see that, we feel free to simply, yet powerfully, share our stories.

Telling our stories = more opened hearts for loving
opened hands for shaking,
opened arms for embracing,
opened doors for welcoming,
opened eyes for seeing,
opened minds for understanding.

All of that, just by sharing our stories.

Our stories matter.
Our stories make us who we are.
Our stories are who we choose to become.

A PRAYER FOR OUR STORIES

Lord,

I embrace my story
I embody my story

     My story does not embody me

I seek the humility to listen more
I seek the courage to share more
  All so I may magnify you more

I am free to become who I am
I am empowered to become who I am
  I choose to become who I am

Tell me your story. I tell you my story.
  New stories. Renew stories. I knew my story.
    My new story.

I have your story. Become your story. Be your story.
  Stories, restore. Restore my story. Story restored.

Repeat.

OUR DIVINE STORIES

Why don't we tell our stories more?
Too afraid? Too ashamed? Too embarrassed?

Sometimes we fear we have too many good things to
say, as if we must hide our joy.
> (soothe the suffering, pity the afflicted,
> shield the joyous . . .)

Our stories matter. We matter.
We are enough. No. Matter. What.

Open our lips
Put a new song in my mouth
I still proclaim
Let us declare
My mouth will tell
I have not restrained my lips
I also will acknowledge
I have told the glad news
I have not concealed
My tongue will tell
I will sing

64

I am prepared to make a defense to anyone
of the hope that is within

What do you *pass* on? What do you pass *on*?

When you tell your stories,
Do you get stuck in the joy and pass on the pain
and hurt?
Do you get stuck in the pain and hurt and pass
on the joy?

Perfect—Latin *Perficere*—"to complete"
Perfection is completeness
(light and darkness, death and life, joy and pain)
Completeness is wholeness
Wholeness is healing
Healing is joy

A PRAYER FOR OUR STORIES

II.

How can I partner with you, God, through prayer and faith, to make sense of, make meaning of my story, ultimately recognizing that your will be done?

I remember your story. I re-member your story.
Born humbly. Lived faithfully. Taught creatively.
Served generously. Suffered unnecessarily.
Died violently. Rose triumphantly.
I remember your story. I re-member your story.

Of new life emerging from lifeless bodies;
Of babies being born from infertile wombs
Of teenagers who slay giants
Of faith, the size of a mustard seed that can move
   mountains.

God may not cause everything in our lives, but God sure can use everything.

Every day, out of the chaos we write into our stories, life and light finds a way. Amen.

We are afflicted in every way, but not crushed; perplexed, but not driven to despair; persecuted, but not forsaken; struck down, but not destroyed; always carrying in the body the death of Jesus, so that the life of Jesus may also be made visible in our bodies. (2 Corinthians 4:8-10)

GOD'S STORY

Words kill, words give life; they're either poison or fruit—you choose. (Proverbs 18:21)

Choose God's story again today. Say yes to God's story again.

Write the healing story into our own life stories and pass it on. Choose to tell the story that laughter will wipe away the tears; light will shatter the darkness and that death is not the end. We are an Easter people. And we cannot be silent. Jesus said, even the stones shall cry out in praise. In the newness of Spring, after the transitions of Fall and the desolation of Winter, and in anticipation of the fullness of Summer, even the trees shout; with each explosion of a new bud, a new blossom, life makes a way again.

Healing can begin when we tell our untold stories.

Choose God's story again today. Say yes to God's story again.

Speak it, sing it, dance it, photograph it, pray it, serve it, write it, work it, heal with it, give it, be it, do it, believe it, tell it!

Choose God's story again today!

PART 7

Giver of Life

DIRECTIONS

When going forward in life, it may seem at times overwhelming and unpredictable, resembling more a winding road with many twists and turns. But looking backward, it always seems like a straight line; it makes sense! I was meant to be in those places at those times. Knowing that God has a purpose for my life (Jeremiah 29:11) keeps me grounded. Knowing that each experience, whether difficult or filled with joy, is an opportunity to learn from and listen to God, gives me confidence, courage, and peace.

Remember forward

Believe backward.

MIRACLES

The same God who
Brought sight to the blind
Breathed new life into the dead
Planted babies into barren wombs
Cast demons into pigs
Commanded the lame to walk
Fed thousands with little
Halted the flow of disease
Walked on water

Is the same God who
Wakes us up each morning
New mercies we see
Breathes new life into the dead marriage,
Broken spirit, wounded soul
Plants seeds of opportunities, of hope, of help,
of grace into
Seemingly infertile situations
Banishes the temptations, the enemies,
the bad company,
By giving us the will and power to say "Go!"

Commands us to wake up, get up,
and choose a new path
Feeds many through willing souls,
unexpected generosity,
Kind gestures, acts
Who brings good news in the hospital, new medicines,
new cures, new understandings,

Miracles surround us every day
Tears that wash away pain
Tears that punctuate joy
A laugh that erupts from our bellies
Touches and hugs that bring comfort and solace
Love that appears in the most unexpected places,
Bringing buoyant life, like oxygen to our lungs

GOD'S AMBULANCE

I've always been struck by the way God provides for animals in nature.

Birds sit perched in the gaping jaws of alligators confidently devouring fleshly remnants caught in their massive teeth. God's dentists.

Elegant white egrets delightfully peck at miniscule insects burrowed
On the backs of cattle in the farmlands of Jamaica. God's helpers.

But the other day when I saw a maimed squirrel struggling to cross my driveway, her two hind legs completely broken, I wondered, where's God's ambulance?

I had such a visceral reaction to this sight. I couldn't even look. Couldn't even continue driving. I know it may sound a little silly, but my heart broke in that moment.

I don't have a profound love for squirrels. My heart broke for the unnecessary suffering that I simply could not bear to see. The strength it took just to drag her body across the driveway. The pain she must have been in. Her body screamed in silence, crippled in agony.

Later that day, I walked down to the driveway wondering if I would see this poor squirrel. Had she finally crossed to the other side? And I did.

After hauling her body, the squirrel lay still, quiet, dead.

No more pain. No more suffering. God's ambulance had arrived.

BORN ANEW

With God's grace we make a choice to be
born anew.
It is a choice that changes everything!

We *see* differently.

Our eyes look to the hills from our own life
valleys, and see that God is the great keeper
of our lives! Watching us constantly, with us,
before us, behind us, beside us. Never slum-
bering. And we see the divine in everything:
in our valleys, in our hilltops, in our enemies,
in ourselves.

We *feel* differently.

We feel empowered to completely surrender
our lives to God. We exercise a radical
obedience, listening for and to God's words,
and following them, so ultimately we each
may be a blessing to others and the world.
We feel free of worry and anxiety because
we remember that God already has a dream
for our lives, and by righteous faith, we live
into that dream, drawing and acting on the
divine power and potential that resides deep
within us, magnificently woven into our
DNA—Emmanuel!

We *act* differently.

We change our ways, our hearts, our minds
away from the world and toward God, today.
We choose transformation. We choose the
story that death is not the end, only a new
beginning; that there is always hope; that
wholeness and healing is attainable and
that new life and power emerges from
the bloodied, beaten, lifeless body of our
experiences.

A PILGRIMAGE TO JOY

Encounter
Entangle
Enrage

Enquire
Enlist
Entreat

Engage
Enact
Endure

Enshrine
Enable
Enliven

Endeavor
Enough

EnJOY!

PART 8

Life of the World to Come

WHAT A VIEW

Ridgeview saved my life. Twice.

I am eternally grateful to this place for the impact it has had on my life. I have a second and a third chance at living because of this place. It's been almost 10 years since I was last there for treatment for major depression. I am no longer where I was. But I am so grateful because who I was then has helped create who I am today. Things happen. Our stories happen. But thank God we have the power to shape them and write the endings.

I proclaim that in the depths of my darkest days, when I was suffocating in the oppressive cloud of depression, lying on a hospital bed, a divine inspiration came downloaded to me in the image of a story. I felt a call, I felt compelled to tell my story of the denial, of the despair, of the desire for death; of the discernment, the deliverance, the discovery, and the delight in the Divine. I am so thankful for that story. And so thankful for the courage to tell it.

Life after the View?

Upon leaving a place like this, whether it be a physical place of healing or a spiritual one, we find ourselves on a precipice with a magnificent Panoramic View laid before us.

All things visible and invisible, seen and unseen.
Predictable unpredictability
Certain uncertainty.

And we open our eyes anew
We stand perched on the ridge in awe-some wonder!
A remarkable landscape of
Rocky terrain where we stumble, fall,
and climb again;
Effortless topography punctuated
with slippery slopes
Oceans of hope in which to bathe
Majestic trees that draw our eyes up toward the
heavens and pull our chests up and out
and vulnerable
A flamboyant fusion of darkness and light
Bursting with the possibilities of joy

Then we surrender
And step off . . .

PRAYER OF SELF-DEDICATION

(Book of Not So Common Prayer)

My heart is drawn to you, my mind is guided by you, my imagination is filled with your words and thoughts of you, your will be done, I am wholly yours, utterly dedicated to you. Use me, I pray, as you will and always to your glory and the welfare of your people, through our Lord and Savior Jesus Christ. Amen.

ASTONISH ME!

I am astonished by many things every day
Astonished that my children don't pick up after
   themselves
Astonished when they do!

Astonished that a maimed squirrel can break my heart

Astonished that breasts provide milk, ducts produce
tears, laughter heals, exercise brings relief, and sometimes pain brings peace

Astonished that bellies are distended by the lack of
food in one part of the world and distended by too
much food in another

Astonished that sometimes they live right beside each
other

Astonished that some grown people deliberately hurt
children, hurt others, hurt themselves

Astonished that pain and mis-love and dis-ease can fester within and urge us to hurt children, hurt others, and hurt ourselves.

Astonished that that same pain and mis-love and dis-ease can point us to God and a new truth and a new peace

II.

Astonished that a bowl of water can quench the desperate thirst of a dog

Astonished that the same water can swell into a wave, a powerful force and completely decimate a village, a people, a soul existence

Astonished when we go forward in life that the path may seem uncertain and weary and dark and unpredictable and when we look back, it is a clear, straight line . . . we were meant to be in those places, at those times, feeling those feelings

Astonished when God appears . . . in the indescribable blue in the dome separating water from land

In the selfless acts of my mother-nurse who picked up children, men and women, so afflicted with sores, poverty, ill-health, the near stench of death, off the streets of Jamaica

Astonished when God speaks to us in a still, clear, purposeful, and truthful voice . . . we only have to listen

III.

Astonished by the old Jamaican proverb "every hoe ha' him stick of bush." God provides for each of us in love, in wholeness, no matter what

Astonished that man and woman and man and man and woman and woman make love and family and homes. Together.

Astonished when a life is conceived. Astonished that God already has a purpose for that life; "before you were formed in the womb I knew you"

Astonished when you pick a ripened mango directly from the tree; its nectar kissed by God's sunshine, sweetened by God's mercy

Astonished when young fertile minds are nourished to do good.

Astonished when young fertile minds are nourished to do evil.

Astonished that there are only 26 letters in the English alphabet and over 1 million words!

Words like *mellifluous*
and *onomatopoeia*
and
if

Astonished that creative minds pluck from these bare bones to create linguistic landscapes bursting with images and stories and images and stories and images and stories

I am astonished by God, the very fact of God, that God is.

Astonished by God's mercy, by God's grace, by God's enduring love

Astonish me, God! Astonish me!

A PRAYER OF AFFIRMATION

My be-loved,

You are co-creator with God.

Together you have the courage, the confidence, and the conviction to be who GOD purposed you to be! May you be a blessing to those you encounter; may you always have praise on your lips; and joy in your heart, because of GOD who gives you life!

Selah!

NEW MORNING, NEW MERCIES

(Ostinato Refrain)

Thank you for this opportunity to love you more, love myself more, and to love others more. Thank you for this opportunity to love you more, love myself more, and to love others more. Thank you for this opportunity to love you more, love myself more, and to love others more. Thank you for this opportunity to love you more, love myself more, and to love others more.